W9-AXA-984

J $14.25
971.27   LeVert, Suzanne
Le   Manitoba

DATE DUE

MR 9 '94			
MR 25 '92			
2/9/93			
MR 05			

EAU CLAIRE DISTRICT LIBRARY

DEMCO

Let's Discover Canada

MANITOBA

by
Suzanne LeVert

George Sheppard
McMaster University
General Editor

CHELSEA HOUSE PUBLISHERS
New York   Philadelphia

81962

EAU CLAIRE DISTRICT LIBRARY

Cover: Crossing the prairie. Railroads have been central to Manitoba's development.
Opposite: A farmers market in Winnipeg, the capital of Manitoba.

Chelsea House Publishers
EDITOR-IN-CHIEF: Remmel Nunn
MANAGING EDITOR: Karyn Gullen Browne
COPY CHIEF: Juliann Barbato
PICTURE EDITOR: Adrian G. Allen
ART DIRECTOR: Maria Epes
DEPUTY COPY CHIEF: Mark Rifkin
ASSISTANT ART DIRECTOR: Noreen Romano
MANUFACTURING MANAGER: Gerald Levine
SYSTEMS MANAGER: Lindsey Ottman
PRODUCTION MANAGER: Joseph Romano
PRODUCTION COORDINATOR: Marie Claire Cebrián

Let's Discover Canada
SENIOR EDITOR: Rebecca Stefoff

Staff for MANITOBA
COPY EDITOR: Benson D. Simmonds
EDITORIAL ASSISTANT: Ian Wilker
PICTURE RESEARCH: Patricia Burns
DESIGNER: Diana Blume

Copyright © 1991 by Chelsea House Publishers, a division of Main Line Book Co. All rights reserved. Printed and bound in the United States of America.

First Printing

1   3   5   7   9   8   6   4   2

Library of Congress Cataloging-in-Publication Data

LeVert, Suzanne
   Let's discover Canada. Manitoba/by Suzanne LeVert; George
Sheppard, general editor.
      p.   cm.
   Summary: Discusses the history, geography, and culture of the
Canadian province of Manitoba.
   Includes bibliographical references and index.
   ISBN 0-7910-1025-2
   1. Manitoba—Juvenile literature. [1. Manitoba.] I. Sheppard.
George C. B. II. Title   90-46034
F1062.4.L48   1991   CIP
971.27—dc20   AC

Contents

My Canada

by Pierre Berton

"Nobody knows my country," a great Canadian journalist, Bruce Hutchison, wrote almost half a century ago. It is still true. Most Americans, I think, see Canada as a pleasant vacationland and not much more. And yet we are the United States's greatest single commercial customer, and the United States is our largest customer.

Lacking a major movie industry, we have made no wide-screen epics to chronicle our triumphs and our tragedies. But then there has been little blood in our colonial past—no revolutions, no civil war, not even a wild west. Yet our history is crammed with remarkable men and women. I am thinking of Joshua Slocum, the first man to sail alone around the world, and Robert Henderson, the prospector who helped start the Klondike gold rush. I am thinking of some of our famous artists and writers—comedian Dan Aykroyd, novelists Margaret Atwood and Robertson Davies, such popular performers as Michael J. Fox, Anne Murray, Gordon Lightfoot, and k.d. lang, and hockey greats from Maurice Richard to Gordie Howe to Wayne Gretzky.

The real shape of Canada explains why our greatest epic has been the building of the Pacific Railway to unite the nation from

sea to sea in 1885. On the map, the country looks square. But because the overwhelming majority of Canadians live within 100 miles (160 kilometers) of the U.S. border, in practical terms the nation is long and skinny. We are in fact an archipelago of population islands separated by implacable barriers—the angry ocean, three mountain walls, and the Canadian Shield, that vast desert of billion-year-old rock that sprawls over half the country, rich in mineral treasures, impossible for agriculture.

Canada's geography makes the country difficult to govern and explains our obsession with transportation and communication. The government has to be as involved in railways, airlines, and broadcasting networks as it is with social services such as universal medical care. Rugged individualism is not a Canadian quality. Given the environment, people long ago learned to work together for security.

It is ironic that the very bulwarks that separate us—the chiseled peaks of the Selkirk Mountains, the gnarled scarps north of Lake Superior, the ice-choked waters of the Northumberland Strait —should also be among our greatest attractions for tourists and artists. But if that is the paradox of Canada, it is also the glory.

Although the tundra of northern Manitoba appears bleak and rugged, it is in reality a fragile ecosystem, easily thrown out of balance by human activity.

CANADA

UNITED STATES

ATLANTIC OCEAN

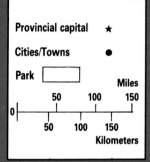

Provincial capital ★

Cities/Towns ●

Park ▭

Miles
0   50   100   150
0   50   100   150
Kilometers

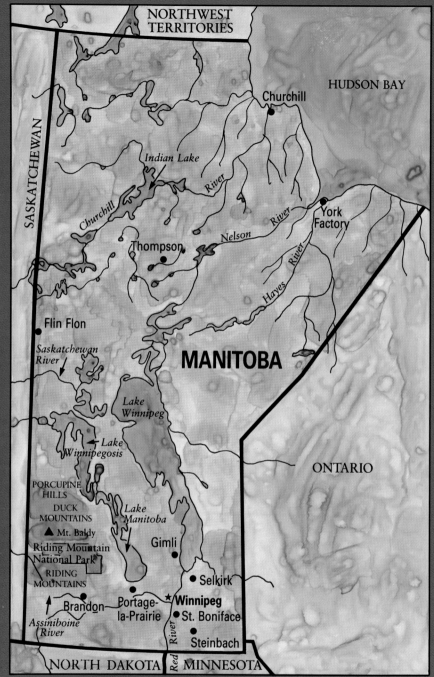

NORTHWEST TERRITORIES

HUDSON BAY

Churchill

SASKATCHEWAN

Indian Lake

Churchill River

Nelson River

Hayes River

York Factory

Thompson

MANITOBA

Flin Flon

Saskatchewan River

Lake Winnipeg

Lake Winnipegosis

ONTARIO

PORCUPINE HILLS

DUCK MOUNTAINS

▲ Mt. Baldy

Lake Manitoba

Gimli

Riding Mountain National Park

RIDING MOUNTAINS

Selkirk

Brandon

Portage-la-Prairie

★ Winnipeg
● St. Boniface

Assiniboine River

Red River

Steinbach

NORTH DAKOTA   MINNESOTA

Pasqueflower

Great gray owl

Manitoba at a Glance

Population: 1,063,016 (1986 census)

Area: 250,947 square miles (649,953 square kilometers)

Capital: Winnipeg (population 594,551)

Other major cities: St. Boniface (96,013), Brandon (38,708)

Major lakes: Winnipeg, Winnipegosis, Manitoba

Highest point: Mt. Baldy, 2,746 feet (837 meters)

Major rivers: Churchill, Nelson, Assiniboine, Red

Entered Dominion of Canada: July 15, 1870

Principal products: Wheat, oats, barley, livestock, nickel, petroleum, copper, gold, zinc, iron and steel products, chemicals, electrical goods

Government: A parliament with a single-house legislature of 57 members, popularly elected by district for terms of 5 years; principal political parties are the Liberals, the Conservatives, and the New Democrats; the formal head of state is the lieutenant governor, who is appointed by Canada's federal government as a representative of the British crown; the head of government is the premier, who is a member of the legislative assembly; Manitoba is represented in the federal government in Ottawa by 6 senators and 14 members of the House of Commons

The Land

A keystone is the stone at the top of an arch that holds the other stones in place; therefore, because it is located near the geographic center of North America and at the heart of Canada, Manitoba has been called Canada's Keystone Province. Manitoba has long served as a major transportation and communications link between eastern and western Canada. It is Canada's sixth largest province, with an area of 250,947 square miles (649,953 square kilometers). It is bordered on the north by the Northwest Territories, on the east by Ontario, on the west by Saskatchewan, and on the south by Minnesota and North Dakota in the United States. In the northeast, Manitoba has 400 miles (640 kilometers) of shoreline along Hudson Bay, a huge inland body of salt water that is connected by various channels to the North Atlantic and Arctic oceans.

Manitoba is the easternmost of Canada's three prairie provinces; the other two are Saskatchewan and Alberta. Although Manitoba is known for its rich soil and flat landscape, it has a variety of resources. In fact, only one-third of Manitoba is prairie land. This region is west of a line that runs from the southeastern

Opposite: Horsemen in Riding Mountain National Park explore the hill-and-lake country of western Manitoba. *Above:* Lake Winnipeg, about 50 miles (80 kilometers) north of the capital, is the province's biggest lake and one of the largest bodies of fresh water in the world.

edge of the province to the city of Flin Flon, on its northwestern border with Saskatchewan. Most of Manitoba's population lives in this part of the province. The rest of Manitoba consists of sparsely populated forest wilderness.

The rocky terrain of northern Manitoba is part of the Canadian Shield, a vast horseshoe-shaped formation of ancient bedrock that underlies almost half of Canada and part of the United States. The Shield contains some of the oldest rock formations in the world—2.7 billion years old. The Canadian Shield is generally not very suitable for farming because of its thin soil and rocky surface, but it has vast stores of mineral ores, including nickel, copper, gold, and zinc.

Regions and Wildlife

During the last Ice Age, enormous glaciers covered most of Manitoba. The retreat of these glaciers more than 10,000 years ago shaped the province's geography. Melting snow and ice scraped the surface of the land, exposing the rocks of the Canadian Shield and carving out powerful rivers and thousands of lakes. In the south, the Ice Age left a different kind of legacy. Meltwater from the glaciers formed a huge body of water called Lake Agassiz. For thousands of years, soil was washed into Lake Agassiz and deposited in layers of fine-grained sediment on the lake bottom. The lake disappeared many years ago, and that sediment is now some of Canada's most agriculturally productive soil. Limestone, gypsum, and clay are also mined from this rich, silty earth.

Manitoba's generally level terrain also was created by the Ice Age. The weight of the glaciers pressing against the earth left the province rather flat. Furthermore, Manitoba was almost unaffected by the mountain-building process that raised western Canada's jagged mountain ranges and lofty peaks. But Manitoba does have a hilly region along its southwestern border. The three main highlands here are called the Porcupine Hills, the Duck Mountains, and the Riding Mountains. Manitoba's highest point is Mt. Baldy in the Ducks; it reaches a height of 2,746 feet (837 meters).

The town of Minnedosa nestles among wheat fields in southwestern Manitoba. Like Saskatchewan and Alberta, Manitoba is a prairie province and an important producer of grain.

The province has three distinct types of terrain: tundra, forest, and prairie. The tundra is the subarctic region in the far north and on the shore of Hudson Bay. This is a frigid, treeless zone where the only plants are small scrub pines, moss, lichens, and others hardy enough to survive the bitter cold and short growing season. South of the tundra is the forest, which covers nearly 63 percent of the province. The northern forest is made up of evergreens such as white and black spruce, larch, fir, and jack pine. In central Manitoba, elm, ash, aspen, Manitoba maple, and oak are mixed with these evergreens. The southern prairie region is characterized by broad, rolling grasslands with scattered clumps of trees.

Buffalo, antelope, and elk once roamed the prairie. They no longer live in the settled and cultivated areas, although deer are still numerous in the south. Gophers, badgers, coyotes, and jackrabbits are now the most common wild animals on the prairie; grouse and ducks are typical birds. Manitoba's larger wildlife is found in its forests. The northern, or boreal, forests are inhabited by caribou, elk, and moose. Black bears and timber wolves can be found throughout central Manitoba. Fur-bearing forest animals, such as beaver, fox, otter, marten, lynx, mink, and muskrat, all shaped Manitoba's history by providing the furs upon which its early economy was built.

Near the town of Churchill on Hudson Bay, a polar bear surveys a realm of water and ice. Churchill is often referred to as the Polar Bear Capital of the World.

Two noteworthy species of mammals are found in the far north, especially near the port of Churchill on Hudson Bay. One is the white beluga whale, a relative of the dolphin. Hundreds of these friendly, intelligent creatures feed at the mouth of the Churchill River during the summer. The other is the polar bear. One of the world's largest communities of polar bears lives just south of Churchill. Snowy white, often dangerous, and capable of swimming long distances, the polar bear is most active during the winter, hibernating for much of the summer.

Rivers and Lakes

More than one-sixth of Manitoba's total area—about 39,225 square miles (101,592 square kilometers)—consists of lakes and rivers. Although many of Manitoba's 100,000 or more lakes have never been mapped or even named, others are among the largest in Canada. Lake Winnipeg is Manitoba's biggest, with an area of 9,465 square miles (24,514 square kilometers), larger than Lake Ontario in the Great Lakes system. It is the world's 13th largest body of fresh water and the largest body of water in North America that is within a single province or state. The province's other major lakes are Winnipegosis, Manitoba, and Indian. Lakes Winnipeg, Winnipegosis, and Manitoba are remnants of Lake Agassiz, which once covered an area greater than that of all three lakes combined.

Manitoba's lakes and rivers form a great waterway and drainage system. One-quarter of all North American fresh water drains through Manitoba into Hudson Bay. Because Manitoba is lower and flatter than the other prairie provinces, it draws water from Canada's western highlands down toward the bay through the Saskatchewan, Churchill, and Nelson rivers. And the Winnipeg, Red, and Assiniboine rivers—together with the province's large lakes—drain a vast region to the south of Manitoba as well.

This abundance of fresh water has had both good and bad effects on Manitoba. On the positive side, the province has some of the most powerful hydroelectric power plants in Canada.

EAU CLAIRE DISTRICT LIBRARY

Dams and power plants along the rivers produce a surplus of energy, which is sold to neighboring provinces and to the United States. But flooding is a problem in many areas because of the province's flat terrain. The worst flooding occurs along the Red River and its principal tributaries, the Souris and the Assiniboine. Major flood control programs have been undertaken, beginning with the Red River Floodway, completed in 1968.

Climate and Weather

A herd of caribou charges across the northern tundra. The caribou, a relative of the reindeer, ranges across arctic North America and Siberia.

Cold, snowy winters and warm, sunny summers make Manitoba's climate one of the most diverse—and invigorating—in Canada. The province has extreme seasonal variations in weather,

Flooding has long been a problem along the southern rivers. In May 1979, the Red River overflowed its banks; people in Winnipeg erected dikes, hoping to save their homes.

especially in the north, where temperatures often plummet to about −17 degrees Fahrenheit (−27 degrees Centigrade) in January and climb to 55°F (13°C) in July. Southern Manitoba is a bit more moderate, with temperatures averaging around 0°F (−18°C) in the depths of winter and 69°F (20°C) in July. Throughout the province, however, these figures may vary widely, especially during the winter, when temperatures can fall or rise dramatically in just a few hours.

Unlike the two prairie provinces to its west, Manitoba usually receives ample rainfall. Annual precipitation averages about 20 inches (50 centimeters) a year. Nearly two-thirds of this falls as rain between May and October; the remainder falls as snow, which tends to be heaviest in the east and diminishes westward. Subarctic conditions prevail over the far north, especially near Hudson Bay, which tends to stay cold even during the summer.

The History

While Ice Age glaciers still covered large portions of Canada, the ancestors of today's Native Americans migrated from Asia to North America. Because no written records were left by these first North American peoples, little is known about them or their way of life. Most scholars believe, however, that the first inhabitants appeared in the region that is now Manitoba about 11,000 or 12,000 years ago.

By the early 17th century, when the first Europeans arrived, five Native groups inhabited the area. Two of these groups lived in the far north. The Inuit, people of the Arctic who speak Inuit or Eskimo-Aleut languages, survived by hunting whales in Hudson Bay and caribou in the boreal forest. Their neighbors and enemies were the Chipewyan, who also hunted caribou. The Chipewyan were probably the first Natives to meet the Europeans, who arrived in Manitoba by way of Hudson Bay.

Just south of the Inuit and Chipewyan lived the Woodland Cree, who hunted and fished in Manitoba's forests and rivers. Central Manitoba was the domain of the Ojibway, a group of tribes closely related to the Cree. The Ojibway lived in dome-

Opposite: Red Bird, a Chipewyan chieftain, was photographed with his wife around 1900. The Chipewyan were one of five Native American peoples who lived in present-day Manitoba when European explorers arrived. *Above:* In an 1889 photograph, Inuit of the far north slaughter beluga whales netted in Hudson Bay. In the 20th century, Inuit hunting and fishing practices have been transformed by the use of rifles, snowmobiles, and outboard motors.

Henry Hudson, the first English mariner to sail into the bay that bears his name, was cast adrift on the bay by mutineers in 1611. This 1881 painting of Hudson and his son is by John Collier.

shaped birch-bark dwellings, clothed themselves in animal skins, and traveled by canoe in summer and by snowshoe in winter. The province's name comes from the Ojibway words *Manitou bau*, which mean Strait of the God—the name they gave to a narrow part of Lake Manitoba.

The flat prairie land of southern Manitoba was the home of the Assiniboine people, who were related to the Sioux of the United States. Buffalo hunting formed the basis of the Assiniboine economy and culture. The Assiniboine were particularly skilled at building efficient buffalo pounds, corrals into which herds were driven and then killed. Products of the buffalo included hides (used to make clothing, tents, moccasins, and shields), horns and bones (carved into tools and weapons), and buffalo dung (dried and burned as fuel on the treeless prairie). Most important was the buffalo meat, which was cooked, dried, or ground up with fat and berries to make pemmican, a staple food of both the Natives and, later, the European pioneers.

Although battles between various tribes were not uncommon, resources and land were so abundant that Natives lived in relative peace and prosperity for centuries. When Europeans arrived in the early 17th century, however, the Natives' traditional ways of life were changed abruptly and forever. The Europeans' desire for wealth and land affected the Native peoples in many ways. Age-old tribal rivalries intensified as tribes competed with each other to trade furs to Europeans for liquor and weapons. Even more devastating were the diseases that Europeans brought to the New World—particularly smallpox and measles, which proved deadly to the Native Americans, who had had no chance to develop immunity to them. The Assiniboine, for example, were nearly wiped out by epidemics during the 19th century. Once flourishing with nearly 10,000 members, the Assiniboine nation numbered just 2,600 in 1890.

A map printed in Amsterdam in 1612 shows an early image of Hudson's discoveries: a channel leading into the North American continent and a long bay (at the left of the map). Later explorers found that the bay did not lead to the hoped-for Northwest Passage.

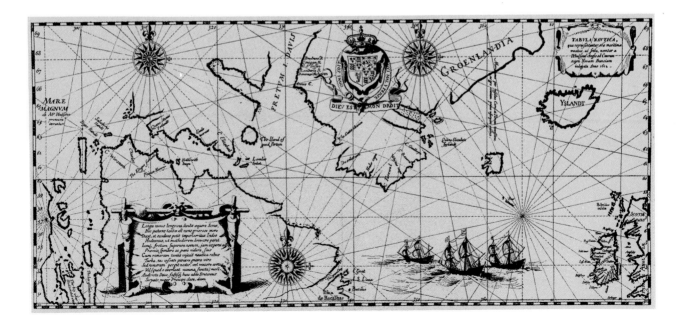

But the greatest threat to Native ways of life was simply the sheer number of Europeans who wanted to settle in Canada. As more and more settlers arrived, forests were cleared, buffalo were slaughtered, and prairie was plowed for agriculture. Native Americans were pushed onto smaller and smaller reserves of land—and out of the mainstream of Canadian life. Today, in Manitoba and throughout Canada, Native Americans are striving to maintain their cultural identities. Native organizations are also fighting to gain political and economic power and to win back, primarily through lawsuits, land they claim was stolen by the Europeans.

The Arrival of the Europeans

The first part of present-day Manitoba to be explored by Europeans was the most inhospitable part, the frigid tundra around Hudson Bay. Nearly a century later, the bounty of the plains was discovered, but many more years passed before permanent agricultural settlements were established.

The search for the fabled Northwest Passage first brought Europeans to Manitoba's shores. Hoping to find a sea passage that would allow European ships to reach Asia through North America, explorers probed the maze of ice-choked channels, straits, and bays west of Greenland. An English explorer, Henry Hudson, braved the chill, unknown waters of northeastern Canada. Sailing with a crew of 21, he reached the bay that now bears his name in 1610. Hudson was probably the first European to catch sight of Manitoba, but he may never have set foot upon its shores. His crew, weary and frightened after a desperate winter, mutinied in the spring. They forced Hudson, his son, and seven others into a small boat and set them adrift in James Bay, an inlet on the southern edge of Hudson Bay.

Hudson was never seen or heard from again, but his rebellious crew made it back to England. The tales they told of the region's great waterways excited other explorers. Thomas Button followed Hudson's route in 1612 and spent the winter at the mouth of the Nelson River on the bay. Jens Munk and Luke

York Factory, on the shore of Hudson Bay, was established as a Hudson's Bay Company trading post in 1682. Although the isolated post was still in operation when this photograph was taken in 1926, it was closed in 1957, after nearly three centuries of serving trappers, traders, and villages in the north.

Fox also searched the bay, still hoping to find a northern waterway to the Pacific. No such waterway from the bay exists, however, and efforts to find one were soon abandoned; the search for the Northwest Passage moved north into the Arctic Ocean. But the exploration of Hudson Bay had not been in vain. Europeans had discovered that it was the gateway to a land of many possibilities. The nations of Europe, particularly France and Britain, competed fiercely for two centuries to control that land.

The Fur Trade

Credit for the early exploration of Canada is due largely to the sleek, warm, waterproof furs of such creatures as the beaver, lynx, fox, and muskrat. Desire for these valuable pelts, which were highly prized in Europe, drove the explorers and traders into the interior of North America.

Ironically, two French adventurers from Montreal were responsible for Britain's strongest claim upon Canadian soil. Without ever visiting the area, Pierre-Esprit Radisson and Médard Chouart des Groseilliers, became convinced that the dense forests south of Hudson Bay were teeming with fur-bearing animals. Unable to persuade their own government of this, they asked the king of England, Charles II, to fund an expedition into the

Lord Selkirk (1771–1820), one of the owners of the Hudson's Bay Company, founded the first agricultural settlement in Manitoba. It was located at the junction of the Red and Assiniboine rivers, where Winnipeg stands today.

territory. One catch of pelts convinced King Charles that the Frenchmen had been right. He established a new fur-trading company and gave it a grant to control a vast amount of land in Canada. The company was founded in 1670 and called the Hudson's Bay Company (HBC); its territory was called Prince Rupert's Land. Eventually, Prince Rupert's Land came to include present-day northern Quebec and Ontario, all of Manitoba, most of Saskatchewan, southern Alberta, and a portion of the Northwest Territories. The Hudson's Bay Company and its agents controlled this expanse for several centuries, establishing some 100 posts across the country.

By 1685, the HBC had established three outposts—Fort Albany, Fort Nelson, and York Factory—along the shores of Hudson and James bays. York Factory was the oldest permanent settlement in what is now Manitoba, and it quickly became the most important post in Canada. Located at the mouth of the Nelson River, York Factory was the hub of the HBC's activity in Prince Rupert's Land. All goods going into and out of the territory passed through it.

The British were not alone in their quest for land and furs. The French, too, had established a successful fur trade in the eastern part of this territory. Refusing to recognize Britain's claim to Prince Rupert's Land, France sent troops to James Bay in 1686. Several HBC forts fell to the French; only York Factory remained in British hands. In 1693, British troops recaptured Fort Albany, but a year later the French gained the upper hand and forced the surrender of York Factory.

Fighting alongside the Europeans were the Native Americans, who had quickly become dependent on the fur trade. The Chipewyan and Assiniboine fought with the British against the Ojibway and Cree, who were allied with the French. For almost 30 years, the territory southeast and west of Hudson Bay passed back and forth between the French and the British. In 1713, the Treaty of Utrecht ended France's claim to much North American territory, including Prince Rupert's Land. Yet the HBC did not go unchallenged after 1713. The French continued to explore and trade in Prince Rupert's Land until the late 1760s. And an even greater threat to the British monopoly came from a group of rival traders who formed the North West Company, based in Montreal. As the HBC moved westward, setting up forts along the way, so too did the North West Company. Not until 1821, when the HBC bought and absorbed the North West Company, did the intense rivalry for pelts finally end.

The Settlement of the Prairies

By 1821, explorers and fur traders had penetrated into the interior of Prince Rupert's Land. Eventually they passed through the forest lands and reached the southern prairies. The first European to see the prairies was probably Henry Kelsey, an agent of the HBC, who traveled down the Hayes and Nelson rivers in 1690.

French fur traders set up a number of posts in what is now southern Manitoba in the early 18th century. The La Vérendrye family, a father and two sons, were largely responsible for the early French settlement of the prairies. In the early 1730s, the family built four forts along the Red River and at the present site of Winnipeg. In addition to promoting the fur trade, the French established close relationships with the local Native Americans.

The Broken Head Mission was one of many lonely missionary outposts that dotted Prince Rupert's Land during the 1850s and 1860s. Roman Catholic and Protestant missionaries operated the region's first schools and hospitals.

Many marriages and liaisons took place between Frenchmen and Native women; their children were called Métis. In generations to come, the Métis became a powerful force in the region.

In 1812, the first British settlement along the Red River was established by a Scottish nobleman, Lord Thomas Selkirk, one of the owners of the HBC. The company gave Selkirk a land grant of 113,000 square miles (292,670 square kilometers) in what is now south-central Manitoba in the hope that he could establish an agricultural settlement there to produce food for the company's western operations. The people of the Red River settlement had a number of fights with the local Assiniboine and also with representatives of the North West Company, as neither the Natives nor the rival traders welcomed the prospect of a permanent HBC settlement. After 1821, when the two trading companies merged, the HBC bought the land grant back from Lord Selkirk's heirs. Many of the early Red River forts in and around Winnipeg are now preserved as national historic sites.

In the early 19th century, a few farmers came from Europe or eastern Canada to join Selkirk's settlers; the trickle of immigrants increased to a flood later in the century. Among the

Louis Riel, shown seated at the center of his revolutionary council, led the Métis of the northwest in two uprisings against the eastern government. He appeared victorious in Manitoba in 1869–70, but a later uprising in Saskatchewan cost him his life.

early arrivals were missionaries—both Roman Catholic and Protestant. They built Manitoba's first schools and churches, institutions that gave the area a sense of community and purpose. But Manitoba's pioneers faced many difficulties. Hard hit by poor weather conditions, including frequent flooding, cold winters, and locust invasions, they lost many harvests. In addition, the settlers were resented by the Métis and the Natives, who viewed with increasing alarm the European expansion into their territory. The settlers attempted, often ruthlessly, to secure the land for themselves while the Métis and Natives tried to defend and assert their claims to the same land.

By the 1860s, it was clear that the far-flung agents of the HBC could no longer oversee the growing population of Prince Rupert's Land. The British feared that the United States would try to take over this loosely held territory, so British officials urged the HBC to sell the territory to the government. At the same time, however, the colonies of eastern Canada were moving toward independence from Britain and the unification of a Canadian nation. Finally, in 1867, the British North America Act established the new Dominion of Canada. At first, the Dominion had four provinces: Ontario, Quebec, New Brunswick, and Nova Scotia. A provision of the Act, however, guaranteed that Prince Rupert's Land would become part of the Dominion as soon as the HBC sold the territory.

In 1869, the Hudson's Bay Company sold Prince Rupert's Land to the governments of Great Britain and Canada in exchange for 300,000 pounds sterling. The sale was to become effective on December 1 of that year. On that date, the Dominion of Canada would take control of Prince Rupert's Land, which was renamed the North West Territories.

The Riel Uprisings

In preparation for its takeover of the North West Territories, the Canadian government sent surveyors into central Manitoba to lay out townships. But the government disregarded the rights of the Métis, who made up about 60 percent of the region's population.

When the surveyors began their work, a group of outraged Métis forced them to stop. The Métis were supported by people of mixed British and Native descent—called "country-born"—and by Native Americans. Their leader was a 25-year-old Métis named Louis Riel. Educated in Montreal, Riel was a shrewd and charismatic man who quickly organized an impressive number of Métis. Throughout the winter of 1869–70, Riel and his followers successfully—sometimes violently—prevented Canada from taking control of their land. They stopped the newly appointed lieutenant governor from taking office and formed their own provisional government with Riel at its head.

Riel's government overreached itself when it captured and executed Thomas Scott, an Ontario farmer who had organized a volunteer brigade to fight the Métis. Scott's execution led to Riel's downfall, for it made the Canadian government quite determined to crush the Métis. In the spring of 1870, Riel gave the Dominion officials a list of demands to be met before the Red River territory would agree to become part of Canada. He insisted that the Métis be given rights to own their land, to use their own languages (French and Native dialects), and to have a role in politics. The Canadians accepted these conditions, and it seemed that the Métis uprising had succeeded. The Manitoba Act of 1870 created a new Canadian province, called Manitoba, in which people of mixed ancestry were guaranteed landownership and cultural rights.

Riel was elected to the Canadian parliament in Ottawa. But his victory was hollow and short-lived. The rights of Métis and Natives were not guaranteed elsewhere in the North West Territories. In addition, the government charged Riel and his men with treason for the execution of Thomas Scott. Riel was forced to flee before British and Canadian troops could capture him. He spent several years in an insane asylum and several more living in the United States before returning to Canada in 1884. He then led a Métis rebellion in what is now Saskatchewan; he was captured by government troops and executed for treason in 1885. Denounced by the government of his time as a villain and a traitor, Riel later came to be regarded by some Canadians as a

The cross-country railroad reached Manitoba in 1882, ushering in an era of growth and prosperity. Immigrants poured into the province to settle the prairies and to build cities and industries.

heroic freedom fighter. There are a number of memorials to him in Manitoba, the site of his first uprising against domination by Canadians of British descent.

Although the Manitoba Act appeared to be a triumph for the Métis, laws later passed by the federal and provincial governments eroded what the Métis had won, especially after immigration from Europe and eastern Canada increased and the Métis became a minority in Manitoba. In 1890, the Manitoba legislature, controlled by settlers from Ontario, outlawed the use of French in schools and within the government. The Métis' language rights were not enforced in Manitoba until 1970.

The 20th Century

Once Manitoba became part of the Dominion, immigration and settlement began in earnest. Between 1870 and 1881, nearly 45,000 settlers, mostly people of British descent from Ontario, arrived to farm Manitoba's fertile prairies. Immigrants came from Europe as well. A large group of Mennonites, German-speaking members of a Protestant sect that opposed violence and war,

In 1884, when this picture was taken, Winnipeg had a population of about 15,000. It was the gateway to western Canada and the largest business and transportation center between Lake Superior and the Rocky Mountains.

came from the Ukraine, a wheat-growing region in western Russia. Another group of pioneers hailed from Iceland. They established a settlement called New Iceland, which became part of Manitoba in 1881. French-speaking settlers from France and the province of Quebec followed, as did Irish, Scottish, and English families. Large numbers of immigrants also arrived from Germany, the Ukraine, Scandinavia, Poland, the Netherlands, Hungary, and Italy.

The early years of the 20th century were a time of growth and prosperity. Manitoba's population was 152,500 in 1890; by 1911, it had grown to 461,400. Manitoba's economy, which was based on wheat production, thrived due both to increases in international and domestic wheat prices and to a decrease in transportation costs. The boom benefited the capital city, Winnipeg. Located at the meeting place of the Red and Assiniboine rivers, Winnipeg was originally a tiny fur-trading post. But the city grew rapidly. It became a center for river shipping, and after Canada's first east-west railroad reached Winnipeg in 1882, it became western Canada's hub for rail transport as well. Factories, stores, and businesses sprang up by the score in Winnipeg to service Manitoba and the other prairie provinces.

Another important development occurred in 1906, when the province's first hydroelectric plant was built at Pinewa, on the Winnipeg River. Other plants were built to generate electricity from water power, and the availability of plentiful, inexpensive hydroelectric power promoted the growth of factories and industries. Therefore, Manitoba has been able to create a diverse economy, one not dependent solely on agriculture.

In 1913, the first of two major depressions hit Manitoba. Wheat prices dropped and freight rates rose. The following year, the Panama Canal opened, allowing goods to be shipped by water from Europe or eastern North America to the west. This was a severe blow to Manitoba, which was no longer the sole gateway to western Canada. World War I made matters worse. Many working men were recruited into military service, and the province's labor pool shrank. Furthermore, the war brought immigration to a halt and also had drastic effects on Manitoba's ethnic groups. Using the war in Europe as an excuse, the English-speaking majority imprisoned many Ukrainians, Poles, Germans, and other Europeans.

Rows of Mounties maintain order on Winnipeg's Main Street in the wake of the violent Winnipeg General Strike of June 1919.

Economic and social conditions remained depressed after the war. In 1919, workers from all over Canada voiced their discontent with the country's economy and government. Calling for major reforms—including widespread unionization and social benefits—the workers conducted strikes. The largest work stoppage in Canada, the Winnipeg General Strike, took place in Manitoba. More than 30,000 workers from all industries left their jobs on May 15, crippling the retail trade, closing factories, and stopping trains. Even public employees, such as policemen, postal workers, and telephone operators, joined in. Calling for better working conditions, higher wages, and the right to negotiate with their employers, the strikers took to the streets of Winnipeg. The federal government was afraid that the strike would spark similar shutdowns in other cities, so authorities ordered the strikers back to work and arrested the movement's leaders. Then, on June 21, federal police charged into a crowd of demonstrators, killing 1 and injuring about 30 others. The Winnipeg General Strike ended four days later when workers were finally forced to return to work. But it left a legacy of bitterness between workers and government leaders. It was many years before the labor movement recovered from this setback.

The economy continued to decline during the 1920s, except for the development of a mining industry in the north. Next, the worldwide Great Depression of the 1930s, combined with a drought that lasted for several years, crippled Manitoba's farming industry. Unemployment was high in the cities as well, as factories and banks went out of business. In addition to the general dissatisfaction and despair felt at this time by most Canadians, Manitobans and other western Canadians had special complaints. They felt that the federal government ignored their particular needs and favored the wealthier and more populated eastern provinces of Ontario and Quebec. During World War II, for instance, the federal government forced the prairie provinces to neglect their manufacturing industries in order to concentrate on agricultural production. Yet the eastern provinces received enormous federal contracts for war materials that enabled them to modernize and expand their factories. This left the eastern provinces in a much better position than the prairie provinces to experience a surge of industrial growth after the war. Many similar policies have colored political life in Manitoba and the other western provinces, causing considerable resentment toward eastern Canada and the federal government.

Manitoba Today

Manitoba has grown slowly but continuously since the middle of the 20th century. Despite its economic problems, the province continues to pursue its goal of balancing agriculture with industry. In the 1980s, attention turned to development of the abundant mineral and forestry resources that exist in the northern part of the province. As in other parts of Canada, though, there is a growing environmental and conservation movement urging that the logging, papermaking, and mining industries should proceed with caution in a region that is, as yet, largely unspoiled.

Elijah Harper, an Ojibway, is a spokesman for the rights of Native Americans in Manitoba and throughout Canada.

Another important issue in contemporary Manitoban politics is Native rights. As in the rest of Canada and the United States, the Native peoples of Manitoba are increasingly vocal and organized. Many of Manitoba's 47,000 Natives belong to organizations that are fighting for political representation and social equality. Record numbers of Natives and Métis—especially from northern communities, where the Native population is most densely concentrated—have been elected to Manitoba's provincial legislature in recent years.

One Manitoban Native has had a dramatic effect on national politics. Elijah Harper, an Ojibway member of the provincial legislature, made national and international news in 1990 when he was the key force in defeating a proposal called the Meech Lake Accord. The accord was a proposed amendment to Canada's constitution that would have granted the province of Quebec and its French-speaking population a special status in Canada. Harper, speaking for Natives throughout the nation, poignantly asked why the people of Quebec should be given special recognition when Native rights had been abused and neglected for so long.

The Economy

For more than two centuries, Manitoba depended largely on natural resources for its economic well-being. Since the mid-20th century, however, the province has been able to expand and diversify from an economy based solely on resources to one that includes manufacturing and industry as well.

A good transportation network is central to Manitoba's economy. The province's communities are connected with each other and with the rest of Canada by more than 4,000 miles (6,400 kilometers) of railroad track and 11,500 miles (18,400 kilometers) of road—mostly in the south, where the majority of the population lives. Today, the rivers and lakes that once served as routes for exploration and supply still link many smaller communities in the isolated north.

Service industries such as education, health care, advertising, transportation, finance, insurance, and real estate are important aspects of Manitoba's economy. The tourism industry is also of growing importance. Visitors enjoy Winnipeg's many urban cultural attractions, and Manitoba's 12 provincial parks and 10

Opposite: In Selkirk, northeast of Winnipeg, a rolling mill produces sheet metal. Mining and metalworking make up a significant part of the province's economy.
Above: Hopper cars carry grain from Manitoba's prairies to markets in the east. The province's location in the center of Canada makes it a natural transportation hub.

Winnipeg's factories and workshops produce furniture, clothing and shoes, and many other consumer goods.

provincial forest reserves attract nature lovers from all over North America. Riding Mountain, the province's only national park, contains a large lake, a golf course, horseback trails, and many other activities.

Manufacturing and Mining

About 1,300 Manitoban manufacturers employ more than 50,000 people and produce approximately $5 billion worth of goods each year. Food and beverage processing account for one-sixth of all manufacturing. Meat packing has long been an important industry in Winnipeg, where Canada's largest stockyard is located.

Aircraft and farm machinery are also produced in Manitoba, earning about $218 million yearly. Other manufactured products include furniture, cement, shoes and clothing, and chemicals. High-technology industries, such as computers and fiber optics, are expanding in Manitoba, with firms located in Winnipeg and its suburbs.

About two percent of Manitoba's total economic production comes from mining and processing minerals. Nickel accounts for about a third of this revenue; copper, zinc, titanium, and gold are also mined in the Canadian Shield region. The most productive mines are located around the northern city of Thompson. Said to be the largest mineral-extraction operation in North America, the Thompson complex includes mining, smelting, and refining facilities. Marble, gravel, sand, and gypsum are quarried as well, especially in southern Manitoba. In 1951, oil was discovered near the town of Virden, southwest of Winnipeg. Hundreds of wells have since been sunk in this part of the province. Although Manitoba's petroleum output is far less than that of Saskatchewan and Alberta, oil plays an increasingly important role in the provincial economy.

Thompson, one of the northernmost towns in the province, is a mining and smelting center, with nickel, copper, and zinc mines and the huge Inco Ltd. smelting plant. Several new mines were opened in northern Manitoba during the 1980s.

One of the reasons for Manitoba's manufacturing strength is that, unlike the other prairie provinces, it has an abundance of water power. Hydroelectricity provides most of the province's energy. A major power source is the lower Nelson River, along which two power plants were constructed in the 1970s. A hydroelectric plant on the Limestone Rapids of the Nelson, scheduled to open in 1992, will be the largest station in Manitoba. The Saskatchewan and Winnipeg rivers also supply power to Manitoba, neighboring provinces, and the United States.

Agriculture

Manitoba's farms produce more than $1 billion worth of goods, or 5 percent of the province's total economic production, each year. Close to 29,000 farms employ 45,000 people and occupy about 19 million acres (7.7 million hectares) of land. Wheat, the most profitable crop, accounts for about 30 percent of all agricultural income. It is grown throughout southern Manitoba, especially in the southwest. Vegetables are grown in the Red

Grain elevators rise from the fields in Cypress River, a small town in the heart of the wheat-growing district.

River valley, which has the warmest temperatures and the longest growing season. Other important field crops are rapeseed, flaxseed, sugar beets, barley, and potatoes.

Livestock ranching earns another $750 million every year. And the province's first industry, fur trading, still makes a healthy contribution to the economy, with approximately 15,000 trappers harvesting the pelts of wild lynx, bobcat, red fox, coyote, and beaver. In Canada, the Winnipeg fur market is second only to that of Montreal.

Like the other prairie provinces, Manitoba has cooperative marketing organizations that were formed to protect farmers from extreme ups and downs in world grain prices. Two of the largest cooperatives are the Manitoba Pool Elevators and United Grain Growers, both of which also handle livestock and other products.

Forestry and Fishing

Although trees cover almost two-thirds of Manitoba, forestry has never been a major provincial industry. Earnings from the logging, papermaking, and lumber industries total about $17 million every year. About half of the forest land is considered commercially productive, but most forestry operations take place in the north. Approximately 55 percent of the province's wood harvest is used by the pulp-and-paper industry. Another 35 percent is processed into lumber, much of which is used by Manitoba's furniture factories.

The fish catch from Hudson Bay and Manitoba's lakes and rivers earns an estimated $20 million annually, with about 2,000 Manitobans working in the commercial fishing industry. The catch consists mostly of pickerel and whitefish. One fish that is highly regarded by Manitobans and visitors alike is the Lake Manitoba goldeye, which is unique to the province and, when smoked, is considered a great delicacy. The fish are processed and marketed by a federally owned agency called the Freshwater Fish Marketing Company, based in Winnipeg. More than 90 percent of Manitoba's fish catch is exported to cities in the northern United States.

The People

Despite Manitoba's enduring reputation as a prairie paradise, relatively few of its citizens choose to live in the countryside today. Since the middle of the 20th century, there has been a steady population shift from rural to urban living. More than 70 percent of Manitobans now live in cities; the rest dwell on farms or in small rural communities. According to Canada's 1986 census, Manitoba's capital, Winnipeg, has a population of 594,551—more than half of the province's total population of 1,063,016.

Manitoba has more ethnic groups among its population than any other province in Canada. It is sometimes called the multicultural province because of the diversity of its cultural heritage. Some 400,000 Manitobans are of British descent. People of German, Italian, Eastern European, and Scandinavian descent are also numerous. Since the 1960s, Manitoba has experienced a surge of immigration from Asian and South American nations as well.

Opposite: A Russian-style church in the town of Sandy Lake is one of many contributions that Ukrainians have made to the culture and history of Manitoba.
Above: Manitobans of Icelandic descent celebrate their heritage at an annual festival in Gimli, on the shore of Lake Winnipeg.

Manitoba's Native Americans make their homes throughout the province, but many of them, especially the Inuit, or members of Arctic tribes, live in the north. Many of Manitoba's French-speaking citizens are descended from the early French colonists of Quebec and Ontario; they are concentrated mainly in St. Boniface, a city on the outskirts of Winnipeg that is said to have Canada's largest French-speaking community outside of Quebec. The province also has a large Ukrainian community, as do the other prairie provinces, and Canada's national Ukrainian Days Festival is celebrated each July in western Manitoba. People of Icelandic origin, descendants of the settlers who founded New Iceland, live in and around Gimli, a city on Lake Winnipeg that holds an Icelandic Festival each August. The Festival du Voyageur, held each February in Winnipeg, celebrates French Canadian culture and the fur-trade era and is the second largest winter festival in Canada. But the largest of Manitoba's many ethnic celebrations is the yearly Folklorama, held each August in Winnipeg. It is a 2-week festival in which the arts, foods, and heritages of nations around the world are presented in more than 40 pavilions.

Education

Manitoba has about 800 public primary and secondary schools to accommodate some 200,000 students. Approximately four percent of primary-school students attend private schools, most of which are religious; these schools receive funds from the government. Schooling for Natives who live on reserves is provided by the federal rather than the provincial government.

Bilingual education has been a challenge to school officials and teachers since the 1970s, when Manitoba's status as a bilingual English-French province was upheld by the courts. French has been reintroduced to the schools, and Franco-Manitobans can now be taught entirely in French. Students who do not speak French but want to learn Canada's second official language can enroll in a special program called French immersion, in which all subjects—even math and science—are

Located in the heart of the capital city, the University of Winnipeg is one of the province's three universities. The others are the University of Manitoba, also in Winnipeg, and Brandon University.

taught in French. Some schools offer similar programs in other languages, such as German and Russian.

Manitoba's high schools offer vocational and technical courses, in addition to their regular curricula. There are several community colleges for postsecondary programs and adult education. The province also has three major universities: Brandon University, the University of Manitoba, and the University of Winnipeg. The University of Manitoba, located in Winnipeg, is by far the largest of the three and is one of Canada's top universities. It offers widely respected degree programs in agriculture, science, medicine, and law, and is affiliated with several smaller regional colleges. About 12,500 full-time and 6,300 part-time students attend the University of Manitoba each year.

Culture and the Arts

Most of Manitoba's cultural attractions are concentrated in Winnipeg. Dance, theater, music, and art thrive in this city, which is considered one of western Canada's most sophisticated urban centers. The Royal Winnipeg Ballet is its most renowned cultural institution. Founded in 1938, it is the second oldest ballet com-

Ballet dancers practice in Winnipeg. The Royal Winnipeg Ballet is one of the most renowned cultural institutions of the prairie provinces.

pany in North America. The company earned the "Royal" in its title in 1953, when Queen Elizabeth II of Great Britain granted it a royal charter. In addition to its regular season from October to May, the company presents a series of free outdoor summer performances in Winnipeg's Assiniboine Park. In addition, audiences elsewhere in Canada and the rest of the world get the chance to see the Royal Winnipeg Ballet during the 20 weeks the company tours each year.

The Winnipeg Symphony Orchestra gave its first concert in 1948 and now gives about 60 performances at Winnipeg's Centennial Concert Hall during its 36-week annual season. The symphony also provides music for both the Royal Winnipeg Ballet and the Manitoba Opera Association. The University of Manitoba's School of Music gives free concerts throughout the year, and each winter the Manitoba Chamber Orchestra gives concerts at Westminster Church in downtown Winnipeg. The Manitoba Music Festival—Canada's largest music competition and festival—is held in Winnipeg every spring, and the Winnipeg Folk Festival is held there in the summer.

Winnipeg has one of North America's leading regional theaters, the Manitoba Theatre Centre, which features Canada's leading performers in a number of plays each winter. During the summer, the Rainbow Stage presents open-air musicals in Kildonan Park. Franco-Manitobans are represented onstage by Le Cercle Moliére, a French-language theater founded in 1925 and believed to be the oldest operating theater group in Canada. A number of smaller companies, such as the Prairie Theatre Exchange and the Gas Station Theatre, perform the works of both international and local playwrights. Of special interest to young people is the Actor's Showcase, which presents plays and shows for children at several locations in and around Winnipeg.

Manitoba has produced many writers, although some of them have lived and worked elsewhere. The essayist, historian, and poet George Woodcock was born in Winnipeg, but spent much of his life in England and British Columbia. His political essays, biographies, and literary criticism have contributed to the intellectual life of Canada for decades. Well-known Manitoban novelists include Gabrielle Roy and Margaret Lawrence.

Manitoba's contribution to pop culture includes the rock group The Guess Who and their many hit songs, such as "American Woman."

Opposite: The Ukrainian Pioneers is one of many paintings by William Kurelek (1927–77) that depict aspects of life in Manitoba.

Lionel LeMoyne Fitzgerald, one of Canada's most renowned landscape painters, came from Winnipeg; in 1932, he became a member of the Group of Seven, an important group of Canadian painters known for their depictions of Canada's landscapes and wildlife. Fitzgerald's work and that of other Canadian and international artists is displayed at the Winnipeg Art Gallery, the third largest gallery in Canada, which houses a collection of traditional and contemporary paintings, as well as the largest collection of Inuit art in the world. In Brandon, Manitoba's second largest city, the Brandon Allied Arts Centre presents new exhibits of paintings, sculptures, and handicrafts each year.

Throughout the province, museums and historical sites celebrate Manitoba's heritage. Winnipeg's Manitoba Museum of Man and Nature explores the natural and human history of the world as well as the province with graphics, specimens, reconstructions, and audiovisual presentations. The B. J. Hall Museum of Natural History at Brandon University is noted for its collection of 400 mounted birds representing 250 species and for exhibits that show northern animals in a setting of ice and snow.

In Portage-la-Prairie, west of Winnipeg, hundreds of artifacts from Manitoba's pioneer days are displayed at the Fort La Reine Museum and Pioneer Village. In Selkirk, between the capital and Lake Winnipeg, is the Lower Fort Garry National Historic Park. Once a central supply post for the fur trade, Fort Garry has been restored so that visitors can catch a glimpse of the province's early history. Historical sites abound in Winnipeg. Among them are the Riel House, which preserves mementos of Louis Riel's life and family, the Kildonan Presbyterian Church, which was completed in 1854 and was the first Presbyterian church in western Canada, and St. Boniface Basilica, the oldest Roman Catholic cathedral in western Canada and the site of Riel's grave.

Sports and Recreation

Manitoba is a sports-loving province, and excitement was high in 1967, when Winnipeg hosted the Pan-American Games, a competition for more than 3,000 athletes from North, Central,

Curling, a sport imported from Scotland, has become widely popular in Canada. The game involves propelling large rounded stones across a rink of ice toward a mark called the tee. These professionals are engaged in a Winnipeg bonspiel, or tournament.

and South America. The city built an Olympic pool, a velodrome (for cyclists), and an enormous track-and-field stadium—facilities that now serve Manitoba's many amateur and professional athletes and their fans.

Like most Canadians, Manitobans love hockey. Many players now active in the National Hockey League, including Bill Ranford, James Patrick, and Ken Wregget, were born in Manitoba. The province is represented in the NHL by the Winnipeg Jets.

Curling, an ice sport brought to Canada from Scotland, is also quite popular in Manitoba. In fact, the Bonspiel, an annual curling event held in Winnipeg, is one of the world's most prestigious such events, attracting curlers from all over North America. Another Scottish contribution to recreation in Manitoba is golf. Manitoba has more golf courses per person than any other province.

Aside from competitive sports, a great many Manitobans spend their free time enjoying the great outdoors. With water so abundant, it is no wonder that rowing, fishing, boating, and swimming are favorite summer activities. Skating, tobogganing, and cross-country skiing warm up the long, cold winters, and ice fishing is another popular winter pastime.

The Cities

Winnipeg

Situated midway between the Atlantic and Pacific oceans and at the geographic center of North America, Manitoba's capital city has been the cornerstone of the development of western Canada. Winnipeg is Canada's fourth largest city, after Montreal, Toronto, and Calgary. It is about 60 miles (96 kilometers) north of Canada's border with the United States and covers approximately 220 square miles (570 square kilometers) at the junction of the Red and Assiniboine rivers. More than half of Manitoba's population lives within the city limits; thousands more live in the surrounding metropolitan area.

Located in the center of one of the world's most productive farming areas, Winnipeg plays a major role in Canada's agricultural industry. The country's largest grain market is the Winnipeg Commodity Exchange. The Canadian Wheat Board and many major grain companies also have their main offices in Winnipeg.

But the city's economy is based on more than agricultural produce. The Winnipeg metropolitan area, with more than a thousand factories, is one of Canada's leading manufacturing centers. Transportation equipment, clothing, processed foods, and

Opposite: The Golden Boy (top center), a youthful symbol of hope, stands atop the dome of Winnipeg's provincial legislature. The building is surrounded by skyscrapers and streetlights, signs of growth and urban development in a province that is working hard to maintain a stable and diverse economy.
Above: In sharp contrast to Winnipeg's metropolitan cityscape, the border town of Flin Flon, with just over 7,200 inhabitants, is typical of Manitoba's outlying rural communities.

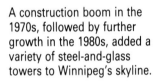
A construction boom in the 1970s, followed by further growth in the 1980s, added a variety of steel-and-glass towers to Winnipeg's skyline.

furniture are among the goods produced in this modern industrial city. The city has one of the country's largest stock exchanges and many banks, making it a financial center as well.

Most important to the city's development has been its position as the gateway for both travel and the shipment of goods between eastern and western Canada. Canada's two transcontinental railroads, the Canadian Pacific Railway and the Canadian National Railways, have their western headquarters in Winnipeg. The Trans-Canada Highway, the 3,020-mile (4,860-kilometer) roadway across the country, passes through the city as well. Winnipeg's International Airport is one of the busiest in the country.

A construction boom during the 1970s added new features to Winnipeg's skyline. Several dozen high-rise office and apartment buildings now tower over the streets of the onetime fur-trading post. A downtown mall called Portage Place, with 150 stores, was completed in the late 1980s. In addition to the new construction, however, Winnipeg has Canada's best collection of century-old office buildings and warehouses. Many of these old buildings are in a neighborhood called the Exchange District, noted for its chic stores and restaurants and its open-air market.

More than 100 parks and nearly 30 golf courses are located in the city, and the Birds Hill Provincial Park is just outside it. During the warmer months, people flock from the city to the broad beaches of Lake Winnipeg, 50 miles (80 kilometers) to the north.

Brandon

Brandon, the major city of southwestern Manitoba, has a population of 38,708. Ever since the Canadian Pacific Railway's transcontinental line was built through the city in the 1880s, Brandon has served as the transportation hub for the surrounding region, including eastern Saskatchewan. Located on the shores of the Assiniboine River, 125 miles (200 kilometers) west of Winnipeg, Brandon is set in a beautiful landscape. The Spruce

Surrounded by wheat fields and cattle ranches, Brandon is the biggest city in western Manitoba. The major east-west rail line passes through the city.

Woods Provincial Forest and the Turtle Mountain Provincial Park are nearby. Despite this pastoral setting, Brandon is an industrial city, with food-processing plants, clothing manufacturers, and petrochemical labs.

It also has a variety of educational and cultural institutions. Brandon University was granted its own charter in 1967, after many years of being affiliated with other colleges and universities. This liberal arts institution has about 3,000 students and specializes in music and music education. The Brandon Allied Arts Centre, a regional library, and many historical museums are among the city's other attractions.

Churchill, Flin Flon, and Portage-la-Prairie

Known as the Polar Bear Capital of the World, Churchill is a cold, isolated community of just 1,217 hardy people. Located on the shores of Hudson Bay about 1,000 miles (1,600 kilometers) north of Winnipeg, Churchill is the only inland seaport in Canada.

The first European to visit the site of what is now Churchill was probably Jens Munk, a Norwegian explorer who searched for the Northwest Passage in 1619. Fur traders lived at a Hudson's Bay Company post on or near Churchill's present-site during the 1700s and 1800s, but it was not until well into the 20th century that the town began to prosper. The completion of the Hudson Bay Railroad terminal and harbor facilities in 1931 paved the way for more than three decades of prosperity for Churchill. In the 1940s, it was a northern supply center and military base. Later, when the federal government built a research station and rocket launching pad there, the population soared to nearly 6,000. Eventually the government cut back on its activities in Churchill, and the community's prosperity and population declined. Most Churchill residents are now employed in either the transportation industry or the growing tourist trade.

Travel agents and tourists have discovered that Churchill offers a rare opportunity to experience the northern wilderness. Every year thousands of visitors come to watch the beluga whales feed at the mouth of the Churchill River or to catch a glimpse of some of the 200 species of migrating birds that nest near Churchill in summer. But the city's most popular—and dangerous—residents are the polar bears. The people of Churchill have learned that tourists from around the world will endure considerable expense and trouble to see and/or photograph these huge, white-furred carnivores—from a safe distance.

Flin Flon and Portage-la-Prairie are typical of Manitoba's small communities; each has a population of about 7,200, although Flin Flon is larger because it extends across the western border into Saskatchewan and includes some Saskatchewan residents as well. Flin Flon is the major town of northwestern Manitoba and has an airfield as well as operations for mining and smelting gold, silver, copper, and zinc. Portage-la-Prairie, west of Winnipeg, is a depot for railway shipping and the home of various engineering and brick-making companies. The town has been shrinking steadily since the 1970s as its young people continue to move away, mostly to Winnipeg.

Although it is one of Manitoba's smallest communities, Churchill is known to people around the world because of the many television shows and magazine articles that have featured the local wildlife. Like much of Canada, the town is a blend of old ways and new technologies, of small-town pioneer spirit and increasingly urban concerns.

Things to Do and See

• **Winnipeg Art Gallery,** Winnipeg: Has many exhibits, including the world's largest collection of art created by the Inuit people of the Arctic, including 6,400 sculptures and 2,000 paintings and drawings.

• **Assiniboine Park,** Winnipeg: Winnipeg's oldest park has 376 acres (152 hectares) of lawns and playgrounds, a zoo, a miniature railway, and both English and French formal gardens. Just south of the park is the Assiniboine Forest, a 692-acre (280-hectare) nature preserve with wildlife and rare wildflowers.

• **The Forks National Historic Site,** south of Winnipeg on the Red River: A park that honors the Natives and settlers who helped build the Canadian west. During the summer, historical exhibits, special events, and children's programs trace Manitoba's unique history. During the winter, the site offers skiing and skating.

• **Museum of Man and Nature,** Winnipeg: One of the foremost interpretive museums in Canada, with seven galleries of dioramas, reconstructions, artifacts, and audiovisual presentations showing the history of man in Manitoba.

Opposite: A hiker and friend pause for a rest in Whiteshell Provincial Park, eastern Manitoba's main recreational and nature park.
Above: Some enthusiastic Manitobans reenact a Viking landing during the Icelandic Festival.

The tomb of Louis Riel, at St. Boniface Basilica in Winnipeg, is one of several historic landmarks that commemorate the leader of the Métis rebellion, now regarded as a folk hero.

• **Ukrainian Cultural and Educational Centre,** Winnipeg: A museum, art gallery, library, archives, and arts and crafts boutique.

• **St. Boniface Centre,** Winnipeg: A celebration of French Canadian culture through art exhibits, craft sales, festivals, music, theater, educational programs, and a French Canadian restaurant.

• **Manitoba Children's Museum,** Winnipeg: Western Canada's first museum for children 2 to 13 years old has hands-on exhibits, including a do-it-yourself television studio and a working locomotive.

• **Wildlife Museum,** Winnipeg: More than 130 preserved specimens of big game from all over the world, including a Kodiak bear, a giraffe, and a Royal Bengal tiger.

• **World's Largest Smoking Pipe,** St. Claude: A functioning pipe 19.7 feet (6 meters) long and 4.9 feet (1.5 meters) high commemorates early settlers who came from Saint-Claude au Jura, France, whose main industry was the manufacture of pipes.

• **Morden and District Museum,** Morden: One of Canada's finest collections of prehistoric marine fossils, some of them 80 million years old, displayed in dioramas and life-size models. Exhibits show the excavation of fossils and the history of the solar system.

• **Spruce Woods Provincial Heritage Park,** Spruce Woods: Stands of spruce and basswood, lakes, and rolling plains make up this park west of Winnipeg. It has a 10-square-mile (25-square-kilometer) tract of sand dunes inhabited by lizards, snakes, and cacti—a little bit of desert on the prairie.

• **International Peace Garden:** Located at the border between Manitoba and North Dakota, this 2,300-acre (930-hectare) garden is dedicated to peace. Each summer the International Music Camp, with weekly sessions in band, choir, orchestra, dance, and drama, is attended by students from all over Canada and the United States.

A diorama at Winnipeg's Museum of Man and Nature shows wolf cubs at play under the watchful eyes of their mother.

• **Eskimo Museum,** Churchill: Located in the Hudson Bay port where many Inuit live, the museum has a fine collection of Inuit carvings and artifacts, including some of the oldest known to exist.

• **York Factory,** southeast of Churchill: The oldest wooden structure still standing on permafrost anywhere in the world is a Hudson's Bay Company depot built in 1832 to replace the original post, which was built in the 1680s. York Factory can be reached only by charter plane or by canoe down the Hayes River.

• **Betula Lake,** Whiteshell Provincial Park: Features large stone figures of turtles, fish, and birds that were used by the Ojibway in traditional ceremonies.

• **Fort Dufferin,** Emerson: Built in 1874 as the first post of the Mounties in Manitoba.

• **St. Anne's Church,** Poplar Point: One of the oldest log churches still used for worship in western Canada.

• **Mennonite Settlement,** Steinbach: Russian Mennonite settlers built more than 50 villages here between 1873 and 1923.

Festivals

Winter: In December, the **Royal Winnipeg Ballet** and the **Winnipeg Symphony Orchestra** present special holiday productions. In January, Winnipeg's **Festival du Voyageur** captures the spirit of the fur-trade era. In February, the **Northern Manitoba Trapper's Festival,** featuring the **World Championship Dogsled Races,** is held in The Pas, and the **Canadian Power Toboggan Championship Races** take place in Beausejour.

Spring: The **Winnipeg International Children's Festival** at the Forks National Historic Site has shows, crafts workshops, puppetry, and other entertainment. The **Royal Manitoba Winter Fair,** with a major livestock exhibition, is held in Brandon in early April. Easter Sunday starts a week of **dogsled racing** in Churchill.

Summer: The **Flin Flon Festival** in June has a canoe race, a month-long fishing derby, and a beauty pageant. The four-day **Winnipeg Folk Festival** in July features gospel, bluegrass, and jazz music performed by international artists. Cowboys and ranchers gather in Morris in July for the **Manitoba Stampede,** called the Big M, with rodeos, chuck wagon races, a parade, and displays of cooking and handicrafts. Another **rodeo** takes place in Swan River in July, and the northern mining town of Thompson celebrates **Nickel Days.** August brings the **National Ukrainian Festival** to Dauphin, the **Islendigadagurinn,** or Icelandic Festival, to Gimli, and **Folklorama** to Winnipeg—not to mention the **Canadian Turtle Derby** races in Boissevain. The **Canadian National Frog Jumping Championships** take place during St. Pierre's **Frog Follies.** Steinbach has **Pioneer Days,** a Mennonite celebration with grain threshing, baking, a horse show, and a barbecue.

Fall: Many towns celebrate **Oktoberfest,** a traditional German festival. In November, Brandon has **Ag-Ex Manitoba,** the province's largest livestock show, with rodeo finals and an indoor truck pull.

Opposite: Morris, a small town in the south, is the site of the Manitoba Stampede, the province's biggest rodeo, held every July.
Below: Cross-country skiers follow a trail at Riding Mountain National Park. Most parks and recreation areas in Manitoba offer similar trails.

Chronology

1610	Henry Hudson sails into Hudson Bay. He is marooned there by his crew.
1682	York Factory is founded by the Hudson's Bay Company (HBC).
1690	Henry Kelsey explores the prairie.
1738	The French build forts near present-day Winnipeg.
1812	Lord Selkirk establishes the HBC's Red River settlement.
1869	Louis Riel leads the Métis in the Red River Rebellion.
1870	Manitoba becomes Canada's fifth province.
1885	Louis Riel leads the Métis and Natives in the North West Rebellion in Saskatchewan and is executed by the government.
1919	The Winnipeg General Strike, the largest in a nationwide outbreak of strikes, ends in a bloody confrontation between workers and police.
1930s	The Great Depression and a drought combine to cripple Manitoba's farming economy.
1970s	Commerce, construction, and manufacturing help diversify the economy during a growth boom.
1972	Winnipeg becomes Canada's third largest city.
1980s	Increased exploitation of mineral and forestry resources is considered.
1990	Elijah Harper, an Ojibway, defeats the Meech Lake Accord, which would have given Quebec special status.

Further Reading

Berton, Pierre. *The Impossible Railway: The Building of the Canadian Pacific.* Magnolia, MA: Peter Smith, 1984.

Coates, Kenneth S., and Fred McGuinness. *The Keystone Province: An Illustrated History of Manitoba Enterprise.* Northridge, CA: Windsor, 1988.

Hocking, Anthony. *Manitoba.* Toronto: McGraw–Hill Ryerson, 1979.

Holbrook, Sabra. *Canada's Kids.* New York: Atheneum, 1983.

Howard, James H. *The Canadian Sioux.* Lincoln: University of Nebraska Press, 1984.

Kurelek, William. *A Prairie Boy's Summer.* Boston: Houghton Mifflin, 1975.

Law, Kevin. *Canada.* New York: Chelsea House, 1990.

McNaught, Kenneth. *The Penguin History of Canada.* New York: Penguin Books, 1988.

Malcolm, Andrew. *The Canadians.* New York: Random House, 1985.

Morton, W. L. *Manitoba: A History.* Toronto: University of Toronto Press, 1967.

Newman, Peter C. *Caesars of the Wilderness: The Story of the Hudson's Bay Company.* New York: Penguin Books, 1988.

———. *The Company of Adventurers.* New York: Viking Penguin, 1985.

Smith, P. J., ed. *The Prairie Provinces.* Toronto: University of Toronto Press, 1972.

Sprague, D. N. *Canada and the Métis: 1869–1885.* Atlantic Highlands, NJ: Humanities, 1988.

Williams, Glyndwr, ed. *Hudson's Bay Miscellany.* Winnipeg: Hudson's Bay Record Society, 1975.

Woodcock, George. *The Canadians.* Cambridge: Harvard University Press, 1980.

Index

ACKNOWLEDGMENTS

The Bettmann Archive: p. 19; Map by Diana Blume: p. 6; Foote Collection, Manitoba Provincial Archives: p. 29; Elijah Harper, NDP Caucus: p. 31; Hudson's Bay Company Archives, Provincial Archives of Manitoba: p. 17; Industry, Science and Technology Canada: cover, pp. 8, 9, 12, 36, 42, 49, 54, 55, 58; © Henry Kalen: pp. 3, 11, 15, 32, 33, 34, 35, 38, 39, 41, 43, 46, 48, 50, 51, 56; By William Kurelek, courtesy the Isaacs Gallery, Toronto: p. 45; © Mike Macri: pp. 5, 14, 53; Manitoba Museum of Man and Nature: p. 57; Manitoba Provincial Archives: pp. 16, 21, 22, 24, 27; Notman Photographic Archives, McCord Museum of Canadian History: pp. 23, 28; Art by Debora Smith: p. 7; Tate Gallery/Art Resource, NY, The Honorable John Collier: p. 18

Suzanne LeVert has contributed several volumes to Chelsea House's LET'S DISCOVER CANADA series. She is the author of four previous books for young readers. One of these, *The Sakharov File*, biography of noted Russian physicist Andrei Sakharov, was selected as a Notable Book by the National Council for the Social Studies. Her other books include *AIDS: In Search of a Killer, The Doubleday Book of Famous Americans*, and *New York*. Ms. LeVert also has extensive experience as an editor, first in children's books at Simon & Schuster, then as associate editor at *Trialogue*, the magazine of the Trilateral Commission, and as senior editor at Save the Children, the international relief and development organization. She lives in Cambridge, Massachusetts.

George Sheppard, General Editor, is a lecturer on Canadian and American history at McMaster University in Hamilton, Ontario. Dr. Sheppard holds an honors B.A. and an M.A. in history from Laurentian University and earned his Ph.D. in Canadian history at McMaster. He has taught Canadian history at Nipissing University in North Bay. His research specialty is the War of 1812, and he has published articles in *Histoire sociale/Social History, Papers of the Bibliographical Society of Canada*, and *Ontario History*. Dr. Sheppard is a native of Timmins, Ontario.

Pierre Berton, Senior Consulting Editor, is the author of 34 books, including *The Mysterious North, Klondike, Great Canadians, The Last Spike, The Great Railway Illustrated, Hollywood's Canada, My Country: The Remarkable Past, The Wild Frontier, The Invasion of Canada, Why We Act Like Canadians, The Klondike Quest*, and *The Arctic Grail*. He has won three Governor General's Awards for creative nonfiction, two National Newspaper Awards, and two ACTRA "Nellies" for broadcasting. He is a Companion of the Order of Canada, a member of the Canadian News Hall of Fame, and holds 12 honorary degrees. Raised in the Yukon, Mr. Berton began his newspaper career in Vancouver. He then became managing editor of *McLean's*, Canada's largest magazine, and subsequently worked for the Canadian Broadcasting Network and the *Toronto Star*. He lives in Kleinburg, Ontario.

EAU CLAIRE DISTRICT LIBRARY